Turning Mistake[...]
Momentum in Business
and in Life

START FROM
EXPERIENCE

Melissa Guenette Mason

❧ LUCKY BOOK PUBLISHING

To request permissions, contact the publisher at hello@luckybookpublishing.com.

For speaking opportunities and consulting inquiries, contact media@alistmediasolutions.com

Paperback ISBN: 978-1-997775-52-2
Hardcover ISBN: 978-1-997775-51-5
E-book ISBN: 978-1-997775-50-8

First edition, November 2025

My Gift to You

I'm beyond thrilled that you're here!

As my gift to you, get FREE access to
the audiobook of *Start From Experience*
by scanning the QR Code below or by visiting
MelissaGuenetteMason.com

Author's Note

This book is called *Start From Experience* because of a screenshot my friend Antonella once sent me. It said: *"You're not starting from scratch, you're starting from experience."* I'm not a sentimental person, but for some reason that phrase stuck with me. I still have it saved on my phone, and I look at it from time to time as a reminder. At the moment I received it, I didn't realize how much I needed those words. They gave me a sense of relief: Everything I had been through, the late nights, the wrong turns, the costly mistakes wasn't wasted. It was preparing me for what came next.

After selling my first company, I wasn't sure if I wanted to go back into business again. I was tired, unsure, and questioning whether I could do it all over. But when I eventually did start another company after my non-compete expired, I realized something important, I wasn't starting from scratch, I was starting with all the lessons my first business had already taught me.

That's what this book is really about. It's not a polished highlight reel. It's a companion full of the things I wish someone had told me earlier. I've filled these chapters with the mistakes I made because those are the parts that no one wants to talk about, but they're the parts you'll learn the most from. My hope is that by sharing them openly, you won't have to pay the same price I did. You can skip the detours, avoid the pitfalls, and move forward with clarity instead of confusion.

Entrepreneurship is one of the loneliest and most challenging paths you can choose. The pressure to look like you have it all together is relentless. But the truth is, no entrepreneur has it all figured out, not at the beginning, not even years in. Everyone stumbles. Everyone doubts. Everyone screws things up. What matters is what you take from those moments. That's why I've written this book as a safe place, one where you can see that struggle doesn't mean failure, it means growth.

And just like me, you're not starting from scratch either. Even if this is your very first step into entrepreneurship, you're carrying years of life experience, skills, and instincts that will serve you. And now, you're carrying mine too.

So as you read, I want you to remember that these chapters aren't just stories, they're shortcuts. They are lessons earned the hard way, given to you so you don't have to repeat them. If this book saves you even one sleepless night, one costly mistake, or one crisis of confidence, then it's done its job.

You're not starting from scratch. You're starting from experience, yours and mine. Together, that is more than enough.

TABLE OF CONTENTS

1
The Rush of the Big Idea

Every great business begins with a spark. That spark becomes fuel, and if nurtured, it grows into a fire that can change everything.

For some, the spark is a bold idea they can't shake. For others, it's a problem they feel compelled to solve. Sometimes it's nothing more than a stubborn belief that things could be better.

That's how my journey began, not with a polished plan or a road map, but with a single spark and the courage to follow it. Even then, I wasn't starting from scratch. I was starting from experience. Every step, every lesson, only made the fire burn stronger.

At twenty-one, I had just moved back home after walking away from what many would have called a dream opportunity in the city. Burned out, unsure of what came next, entrepreneurship wasn't even on my radar.

Then came a turning point. I ran into a friend who owned a restaurant. The food was incredible, the best I'd ever had locally, yet the place was empty. The problem wasn't quality. The problem was invisibility. Nobody knew it existed.

Without hesitation, I said the words that changed everything:

"I can help put you on the map."

It wasn't a business plan. It wasn't a pitch. It was instinct. I just wanted to help. So I threw myself into it, pulling from whatever life experience I had working with people, solving problems, understanding how visibility makes or breaks good work. And it worked. The campaign gave the restaurant a boost. People started showing up.

Then something unexpected happened, other business owners started asking me to help them as well. Suddenly, I had clients. The only problem? I didn't have a business. No name. No pricing model. No contracts. No plan. Just late nights, caffeine, and momentum.

Most people would have said no. But at twenty-one, I was blissfully delusional. I picked a name, built a quick website, and set prices that made no sense. When I didn't know how to do something, I taught myself overnight. And somehow, it worked.

A few months later, the cracks began to show. No systems. No strategy. Just enthusiasm and guesswork. That mix carried me further than I imagined... but also straight into lessons I never saw coming.

Meanwhile, the doubts around me grew louder. Friends

and family believed the safe path was school, a steady job, and a pension. So when I told them I was walking away from stability to chase something that didn't technically exist yet, skepticism filled the room. It wasn't that they didn't believe in me, it was fear. And the unfortunate thing about fear is that it spreads.

Their doubts became my doubts. Maybe they were right. Maybe I was reckless. Maybe this would end badly.

But here's what I knew: When I set my mind to something, I find a way. I wasn't the smartest person in the room, but I was creative, and I was willing to outwork everyone else and that combination became my edge.

That was my first real lesson in business: You don't need all the answers to start. You only need the experience you already have, and the determination to use it.

That mix of creativity, relentless work, and just enough delusion to say yes before knowing the steps became the foundation for everything that followed. And it all started with a restaurant nobody knew about, and someone who didn't know it couldn't be done.

Lesson: You're Never Starting From Scratch

Excitement will push you forward, but it always arrives with fear, your own, and everyone else's. What matters is remembering you already have tools to lean on. Even at the very beginning, you're not starting from nothing. You're starting with every bit of experience you've already lived.

....

Reflection Exercise

Take a few minutes to write down your own experiences you can lean on:

- What challenges have given you grit or resilience?

- What skills, inside or outside of work, could become strengths in your business?

- Whose skepticism is really fear of the unknown, and how can you separate that from your own voice?

2
Clients, Cash, and Chaos

I never went to business school. Most of what I learned came the hard way, through trial, error, and plenty of sleepless nights. But those lessons became the foundation I still rely on today. They're the reason I'm writing this book. The book I wish I could have read at the beginning of my wild journey.

Something every entrepreneur discovers quickly, is that growth without systems isn't progress, it's chaos.

At first, everything was falling into place. One client turned into two, then ten, then twenty. On paper, I had momentum. I was "in business." But I made a mistake that almost every new entrepreneur makes; I thought success meant saying yes to everyone. I never asked if they were the right clients, if their values aligned with mine, or if I even wanted to work with them.

The lessons came quickly. Not all clients are created equal. Some energized me. Others drained me. Some treated me like a partner while others treated me like hired help. Every tough client made me sharper about who I wanted to work with. I learnt that every time you take on a client who isn't a good fit, you're filling space that could have gone to one that does. Saying no became just as powerful as saying yes.

But the real chaos wasn't just in client choices. It was in how I ran the business. Incomplete contracts, no systems and no real pricing model. Payments came in unpredictably, projects dragged, and I was winging it more than I admitted. "Learning by doing" often meant "learning the hard way." While most people didn't notice, I was barely hanging on.

My answer was to hire employees. It sounded responsible and like the next logical step forward. That's what everyone tells you to do when business picks up, but I learned quickly that hiring people isn't the same as leading them. Without systems, clear expectations, or proper training, I wasn't setting anyone up for success. I was handing them chaos and calling it opportunity.

They wanted to do well. I could see it in the long hours, the quiet hesitation before asking questions, the constant effort to meet unclear expectations, but enthusiasm can't replace direction. They didn't have the tools or guidance they needed, and I was too busy putting out fires to build the foundation they deserved.

It's easy to blame the team when things fall apart and

to think they're not fast enough, skilled enough, or committed enough. That isn't the case. A struggling team is a reflection of its leadership. Every missed detail, every bit of confusion, every burnout moment was holding up a mirror to me. If they couldn't rise, it wasn't because they weren't capable, it was because I hadn't yet learned how to lead in a way that lifted everyone with me.

That's when I discovered that hiring too early, before you have a foundation, creates more chaos than it solves. Building a solid team takes time, strategic planning and trust. Payroll isn't just numbers on a spreadsheet, it's trust. People depend on you, and their families depend on you. The responsibility is real, and it should never be taken lightly.

On the surface, I had amazing clients, employees and excellent growth. Behind the scenes, I was stretched thin, but what I didn't know at the time is that every challenge was sharpening me. I was learning lessons no classroom could ever teach. I was learning how to lead, how to prioritize, and how to slow down when speed was breaking everything.

The turning point came when I finally forced myself to slow down. I started turning away clients, not because I didn't want the business, but because I knew that taking on more without a foundation would eventually cause everything to collapse. It's impossible for one person to do it all, and just as impossible to build a business on chaos. Pressing pause was uncomfortable, but necessary. It gave me space to create stability, to put real systems, policies, and procedures in place. By doing this, I gave my team the tools they needed to succeed, which, in turn, gave the business the structure it needed to grow.

As I'm sure you know, businesses can't work without financial structure. In the beginning, I ran everything out of a single personal account with no accountant, no payroll, no reserves. It caught up quickly. Year-end was chaos, tax season was terrifying, and I wasn't just stressed about clients anymore, I was stressed about the government.

Hiring an accountant was one of the best decisions I ever made. I only wish I'd done it sooner. For too long, I ran on hope, telling myself things would "even out next month." But that kind of thinking catches up with you. Once I brought in help, the pressure lifted. Numbers stopped being something to be feared, they became something I could use.

I learned to always know my numbers. Not just what's in the bank, but what's coming in, what's going out, and what needs to stay put. When you know your numbers, you can make calm, confident decisions instead of reactive ones. It's not about obsessing over spreadsheets, it's about creating clarity. And that clarity builds trust. My team knows I'll keep the business steady, even when things shift. That kind of consistency matters more than anything.

Today, that experience has completely reshaped the way I view hiring. My employees are like family to me. I care deeply about them and I'm grateful for the effort they put into my business every single day.

....

Lesson: Growth Without Systems Leads to Stress

Clients are exciting, but growth without structure can bury you. Before you hire, ask yourself:

- Do I have processes in place to train someone effectively?

- Do I truly understand my cash flow, not just my sales?

- Am I taking on clients who align with my values and business vision?

- Can I cover payroll for at least a few months without panicking?

If the answer is no, your job isn't to grow. Your job is to fix the foundation.

Reflection Exercise

Think about your current workload. Which tasks could realistically be delegated if you had the right systems in place?

Look at your finances: Could you confidently make payroll if you hired someone tomorrow? For how long?

What values do you want every employee to understand about your business before they start?

What values should your clients share with you, so the work energizes you instead of draining you?

3
The Glamorous Illusion

People assume being an entrepreneur means freedom to work when you want, where you want. And in some ways, that's true. The catch? Sometimes "working where you want" means answering emails from a bathroom stall at your cousin's wedding, and "working when you want" means all the time.

Part of the problem is what we're shown. The big-name entrepreneurs with bestselling books and massive podcasts love to talk about how their businesses run without them. And that's great, for them. But when you're just starting out, that isn't reality yet. You might not have systems, staff, or cash flow that lets you step away. You're still building. And that doesn't mean you're failing, it just means you're in the stage no one glamorizes: the messy middle.

From the outside, it often looked like I was thriving. Networking events, clients, employees, and a growing business. Social media made it all look polished, but behind the curtain, the pressure was heavy. I felt like I had to wear the mask of success, because what if clients lost confidence? What if employees panicked? What if the people who doubted me from the start finally got to say, "I told you so"?

That mask creates a different kind of loneliness. It's not just being busy, but being unable to tell the truth. Even surrounded by people, you can feel completely isolated, because no one really knows how heavy it is. And when you're the one carrying the responsibility for every client, every employee, every dollar, and every decision, it can feel like there's no safe place to put that weight down.

My friends and family tried to support me, but they couldn't really understand. They had one role at their jobs; I wore twelve hats at once. I was the CEO, the CFO, the HR department, the janitor, the marketer, and the customer service rep, all rolled into one. To this day, I'm not sure my family could clearly describe what I do. They know "I work with the media" or "I throw events" or "I help businesses solve problems" but the actual responsibility, pressure, and language of what I do? It's outside their world.

The mask of loneliness wasn't just at work, I carried it with me everywhere. My friends and family couldn't understand why I couldn't always show up for birthdays, milestones or long weekends. They had sick days, vacation days, and statutory holidays. I didn't. If I stepped away, there was no one waiting in the wings to

keep things moving. Even when I was physically present, my mind was still at work, running through invoices, deadlines, or the next crisis waiting in my inbox. The guilt of missing moments piled up quietly, one skipped dinner or unanswered message at a time. I knew it was temporary, that I was doing it "for the future." But in chasing the business I was building, I often missed the life I was living. This feeling was often hard to explain to those I loved.

The good news is, you don't have to do it alone. One of the best things you can do early is find even one other entrepreneur you can be fully honest with. It doesn't have to be formal, it could be a coffee chat, a brainstorm, or even an online group. That one relationship can change the way you see your own progress.

That's exactly what saved me. When I found friends who were entrepreneurs as well, I didn't need the mask anymore. They already knew what it felt like to juggle everything, to live without weekends, to travel without sightseeing. They understood the loneliness, the pressure, and the exhaustion, and they didn't need me to explain it.

The beautiful part is that I learned from their experiences just as much as they learned from mine. We compared notes, swapped stories, and shared strategies that made us all stronger. That give-and-take reminded me that experience is the most valuable thing we bring to the

table and that it grows even faster when we share it.

So as you read this, consider me one of your entrepreneurial friends. I've been through the messy middle, I've worn the mask, I've made the mistakes. And now, I'm pulling back the curtain so you can learn from my experience the same way I learned from others. You don't have to figure it all out alone.

Those friendships gave me perspective. For the first time, I realized I wasn't behind. I wasn't failing. In fact, I was doing far better than I gave myself credit for. While I was busy comparing myself to everyone else's highlight reel, my entrepreneurial friends helped me see that I was already ahead of where I thought I was.

Behind the sparkly illusions, entrepreneurship will test your mental health, your patience, and your resilience. But it will also give you strength, creativity, and experiences that build you into someone who can handle more than you ever thought possible.

Lesson: Success Without Peace Is Failure in Disguise

- The highlight reel you see online is not reality. Don't measure yourself against it.

- Early-stage entrepreneurship isn't supposed to

look polished, it's about learning, building, and surviving the messy middle.

- True strength is admitting when you need help, not pretending you don't.

Reflection Exercise

- Where in your life are you "wearing the mask" and projecting success you don't feel?

- Who could you be more honest with about your struggles?

- What one small action could you take this week to protect your mental health and give yourself credit for progress?

Closing Thought

Entrepreneurship may look glamorous from the outside, but the real magic isn't in skipping to the end. It's in surviving the messy middle and to appreciating the stage where you're building, learning, and stacking experience that will eventually give you freedom. And when you find people who understand the journey, you realize you're not failing, you're just starting from experience and gaining even more each day.

4
Giving Yourself Grace

Entrepreneurs are taught to hustle, to grind, to "sleep when you're dead." But hustle alone doesn't build a business. Grace does.

Without grace, burnout wins. With it, you last long enough to win.

I see how hard you work, even if you don't. The long hours, the weekend sacrifices and the juggling act no one else notices. You've pulled off miracles most people couldn't imagine, and yet, you probably don't give yourself credit. More often than not, you're your own harshest critic. Please let me say it clearly: You are already doing enough.

When I was starting out, I believed every hour had to be productive. If I wasn't chasing clients or answering emails, I felt guilty. Rest felt like failure. When burnout finally hit, I realized the model I built didn't leave room for me as a human being. That was my wake-up call.

Grace became my strategy. Grace meant saying no to

misaligned clients. Grace meant resting without guilt. Grace meant seeing mistakes not as failure, but as evidence that I was still learning. The irony? The more grace I gave myself, the stronger my business became.

Unfortunately, guilt has a way of sneaking in. I felt guilty for leaving the office early, guilty for saying no, guilty for missing a single email. These standards I had set for myself were not realistic and the sky never fell from taking a break. But guilt didn't just live in my head; it lived in my body with sleepless nights, tight shoulders, knots in my stomach. This guilt didn't make me better, it made me worse.

The first time I gave myself real permission to take a break changed everything. A weekend away, a day without the laptop, I expected disaster. Instead, I came back sharper. Problems that felt impossible on Friday looked manageable by Monday. That's when I understood that pausing isn't laziness. It's strategy.

The paradox of entrepreneurship is a unique one: The more grace you give yourself, the stronger your business becomes. When you protect your energy, you show up sharper for clients, family, and stronger for your vision. Grace doesn't just make your life better, it makes your work better.

Grace doesn't happen by accident. You have to practice it. I kept a "permission list" of things I was allowed to do without guilt: rest, say no, take time for myself. I scheduled downtime with the same seriousness as meetings, because if I didn't protect it, it disappeared. I replaced guilt with gratitude. Instead of thinking, "I shouldn't be resting," I reminded myself, "I'm grateful I'm recharging so I can keep going."

I know it isn't easy, especially in the early years when the stakes feel impossibly high. But I can promise you that giving yourself grace doesn't slow you down. It keeps you in the game long enough to win.

Lessons from Experience

Grace isn't slowing down, it's the fuel that keeps you in the game. Without it, burnout wins. With it, you build a business that allows you to thrive.

Reflection Exercise

Write down three areas where you're hardest on yourself. Reframe each into a statement of grace.

- "I'm failing because I need a break" → "I'm strong enough to rest so I can keep going."

- "I'm weak because I made a mistake" → "I'm

learning, and that makes me stronger."

- "I should be further ahead" → "I'm exactly where I need to be to gain the experience I'll use later."

....

Closing Thought

You don't have to earn rest. You don't have to earn grace. You need them. They aren't indulgence, they're strategy. And when you practice them, you don't just survive this journey. You win it.

5
Moving the Needle

Success in business isn't about doing everything. It's about moving the one needle that matters most.

For finance, that needle is numbers and margins. For sales, it's closing deals. For marketing, it's visibility and reach. For a small business owner, it might be as simple as more customers walking through the door, or one big order that pays the bills for the month. Your job isn't to move every needle. It's to find out which one matters most to the person in front of you, and move it in a way that makes a difference.

In the beginning, I didn't understand that. I tried to fix everything I thought could be improved in a client's business. I carried my own checklist of what "should" be done, and I worked day and night to deliver it all, but I wasn't their CFO, their COO, or their CEO. I didn't get to decide what mattered most. They did. Just because I could help, doesn't mean I should take on more work and problems than I was hired to solve.

The shift happened when I changed the question. Instead of asking, "What do you need?" I started asking, "What does success look like to you?" That one question changed everything. It forced clarity. It revealed priorities. And it gave me a target I could actually hit.

I discovered that clients aren't hiring you to do everything. They're hiring you to move their needle. A homeowner doesn't necessarily want their whole plumbing system rebuilt, they usually just want hot water back before dinner. A bride ordering a cake doesn't care how many recipes you tested, she wants it picture-perfect on her wedding day. A shop owner doesn't want a complete rebrand, they want more customers in the door next month. When you figure out which "needle" matters most, the path forward becomes much clearer.

I found that most of the time, client satisfaction isn't only about the result, it's about how your work makes them look and feel in their own world. Sometimes it's helping them impress their boss. Sometimes it's helping them deliver for their family. Sometimes it's simply making their customers happy. When you do that, you don't just solve a problem. You give them credibility, peace of mind, and a win that matters. That's when you stop being a service provider and start becoming a trusted partner.

Looking back, even the times I missed the mark were valuable. Every tough client, every missed expectation, every hard conversation taught me to ask better questions, to listen closely, and to align my work with what mattered most to them. That's the beauty of starting from experience: You don't have to get it perfect. You just have to keep learning and adjusting until you do.

Lessons from Experience

The fastest way to win with clients is alignment. Don't chase every task. Don't drown in your own priorities. Focus on the one needle that matters most to them, and move it with excellence.

Reflection Exercise

Think back to your last client, project, or even your current boss:

- What was the one needle they cared most about moving?

- Did you define success through their lens, or yours?

- How would your results have shifted if you had asked, *"What does success look like to you?"* upfront?

Closing Thought

At its core, client success isn't about doing more. It's about doing what matters most. When you move the right needle, you don't just deliver results, you build trust, credibility, and staying power. That's when you stop chasing clients and start becoming the partner they can't imagine working without.

6
Building Your Network and Your Net Worth

Networking has a bad reputation, doesn't it? You're probably picturing awkward small talk, a stack of business cards you'll never look at again, and smiling politely over lukewarm appetizers. I get it, I've been there too. However, real networking, the kind that actually grows your business and opens doors years later, isn't about any of that. It's about connection, reputation, and trust.

I learned just how powerful that is when I sold my first business. The buyer wasn't just paying for my company's net worth, they were paying for my network. The relationships I'd built, the credibility I had earned, and the doors those connections could open were worth more than anything on paper. That's when I truly understood the saying "your network is your net worth."

Set yourself up for success. Networking doesn't have to feel fake, in fact, it can be a lot of fun. One of my favorite strategies is to bring a "cheerleader." Having someone else introduce you and sing your praises instantly qualifies you in the eyes of others, and makes your skills more credible than if you had to say it yourself. And of course, you can return the favor for them. It takes the pressure off and makes the whole event feel more like a team sport.

You are going to want to make sure that you don't fall into the trap that I did in the beginning with networking. I often went to the same events with the same people because that is where I felt comfortable. At this point, I wasn't networking anymore, I was socializing and framing it as networking. While it felt good knowing everyone in the room, it wasn't growing my opportunities. To make new rooms more fun, I gamefied it for myself and my employees with a simple rule, that at every event, we must each come back with three new contacts. Not just conversations, real connections with details exchanged. Follow up with a short, genuine message "It was great meeting you, I loved hearing about what you do" is often what makes you stand out in their memory.

Another small but powerful trick is to wear something memorable. Funky glasses, bold shoes, a bright blazer, anything that makes people say, "Oh, you were the one with..." They may forget your name, but they'll remember your signature look, which makes follow-up much easier.

This took practice, I wasn't always this comfortable. I

was a shy kid growing up, the quiet one in class who barely spoke, the quiet one on the playground who kept to themselves. Networking didn't come naturally to me. What helped was starting small. Instead of throwing myself into massive conferences, I went to smaller events with 50 or so people, and I always made sure to arrive early. At that point, the host and a handful of attendees were usually milling around. It made conversations easier and less intimidating. By the time the heavy hitters walked in, it already looked like I knew everyone in the room. Over time, those small steps built my confidence, and eventually, I went from that shy kid to someone who now speaks on large stages, presents in top boardrooms, and built a network strong enough to sell a company on.

One of the most overlooked things about networking is that it's not just about the executives in the room. Some of the most important connections you'll ever make are with the people others ignore; such as the receptionist, the doorman, the bartender. I make it a point to treat everyone with kindness and respect because they are all interesting people and make events a lot more fun.

I'll never forget one receptionist I used to bring coffee to. At the time, she wasn't in a position to help me, but years later, after a shift in the economy, she became the manager of an account I wanted. Out of all the candidates, she chose me, not because I was the flashiest, but because I had treated her with respect when no one else was paying attention. That moment taught me that kindness always compounds.

I hear it all the time that "you have to lead with value" in order to ask someone for their time. I think this is a big misconception. You don't always have to give value in a flashy way for people to want to connect with you. Sometimes, you just have to ask nicely. The best thing a fellow entrepreneur can do is give their time. Successful people understand this better than most. I vividly remember being the young entrepreneur who desperately wanted someone I respected to have a coffee with me. I wanted someone to listen, let me ask questions and because of those coffees, I got to learn from them and build genuine contacts. I've since ended up working with some of those great connections, all because I asked. I will never forget how much that meant to me. Now that I'm in a position to do the same for others, I try to. Not because there's anything in it for me, but because it's the right thing to do. People remember how you make them feel, even years later. That is the real foundation of a powerful network.

Over time, these little practices compound. One introduction leads to another. Someone you met years ago suddenly opens a door you never expected. And if you treat people well along the way and show genuine interest, your reputation becomes a currency all its own.

That's the kind of network that not only grows your business but sustains it through every high and low.

Lessons from Experience

- **Bring a Cheerleader.** Pair up with a friend to validate each other.

- **Set the Three-Contact Rule.** Always leave with three new connections and follow up within 24 hours.

- **Wear an Identifier.** Give people an easy way to remember you.

- **Start Small, Arrive Early.** Smaller events and early arrivals create easier opportunities for real conversations.

- **Lead with Kindness.** Treat everyone with respect

Reflection Exercise

- Who are three people you could reconnect with this week? Reach out with a short message.

- What's one identifier you could wear to your next event?

- Think of one "overlooked" person (a server, receptionist, or junior staffer) you can show kindness to this month.

··

Closing Thought

Your net worth isn't just measured in dollars, it's in people. Every introduction, every follow-up, every act of kindness adds up. Opportunities don't come out of nowhere; they come from relationships. And the stronger your network, the stronger your future.

7
Figuring Out Your Worth

One of the hardest lessons in business is learning to put a price on yourself.

The first time I was asked for a quote, I froze. I hadn't thought about what my work was worth, or how much time and energy each project would actually take. So I did what any 21-year-old without a clue would do, I blurted out a number and prayed they wouldn't laugh.

I quoted from a place of emotion, not logic. I wanted to help these businesses, and I knew they were often struggling, so I underpriced myself. I learnt quickly that empathy doesn't pay your rent. It doesn't cover your bills, your sleep, your internet, or the thousands of invisible costs that come with running a business. It certainly doesn't leave room for growth.

Underpricing while overdelivering was my first big mistake. And while it sounds noble, it doesn't just hurt you, it undervalues your industry, sets false expectations for clients, and makes it harder for the people who *are* charging fairly.

The wake-up call came fast, and I will forever be grateful for the embarrassment that follows. I was still new to business, and at the time, this was the largest company that had ever reached out to me for a quote. I was honoured, nervous and thrilled. I met with the owner, I thought everything was going really well and convinced I had the contract. I awkwardly gave him my quote and then my fear became true, he actually laughed.

Realising I was confused, he politely gave me the brutal truth. He didn't laugh because the price I gave was too high, but because it was comically way too low. Instantly upon hearing the number, he assumed I couldn't be good at my job. He had already spoken to two other firms, both of whom quoted ten times my price. My number was so far off that it damaged my credibility before I even had the chance to prove myself.

That moment stung deep. I can still picture the room, the smell of whisky on the table, even the look on his face. It shook me so much that it forced me to re-evaluate everything I thought I knew about pricing. I realized something that took me years to embody: I wasn't just charging for my hours, I also had to charge for my experience, my creativity, and the results I could deliver. I never got the contract but the valuable lesson was worth far more.

Quoting fairly isn't about greed. It's about sustainability. You have to charge for growth, because if you only ever price to cover today's expenses, your business will never move forward. You need room to invest, to weather the slow months, and to take the risks that make real progress possible. Once I slowed down long enough to really look at my pricing, everything shifted. I researched the market. I tracked the outcomes I was creating for clients. I began to see my own value clearly and I priced accordingly.

I was surprised to realise that when I raised my rates, I didn't lose clients. I gained better ones.

The debate about pricing is one that I have often struggled with. In the early days, most of my clients were small business owners. Working with them was rewarding, but also stressful. The smaller the business, the more emotionally invested the owner was in every decision. Their fear rubbed off on me. Every time they panicked, I panicked. Every time they doubted, I doubted. And because I hadn't yet discovered my worth, I didn't have the confidence to remind them that I was the expert. Instead, I let their fear steer the work.

But when I started charging fairly, I attracted larger clients. They weren't hiring me out of fear, they were hiring me out of trust. They weren't anxious about every tiny detail. They just wanted results. And when I delivered, they were thrilled. No hand-holding. No endless revisions.

Just relief that their problem was solved.

That's when I understood something about the psychology of pricing your work. It isn't just about money. It's about confidence, boundaries, and the kind of clients you attract. Undervaluing yourself doesn't just drain your bank account, it fills your business with fear and chaos. Owning your worth gives you freedom. It attracts clients who respect you, and it allows you to build a business you actually enjoy.

Your pricing should grow with your experience. In the beginning, it's natural to charge less because you're still learning, still finding your footing, and in many ways, your early clients are getting a discount while you figure things out. But once you can deliver with confidence and less guesswork, it's time to re-evaluate.

Yes, raising your rates might mean losing a few clients. But what you gain is so much more valuable: freedom, peace of mind, and the ability to focus on quality over quantity. That shift alone can change everything about how you work and how much you actually enjoy it.

Reflection Exercise

Think back to the last time you underpriced yourself. What hidden costs did you overlook?

- Write down three ways your work adds value beyond just your time. (Examples: expertise, problem-solving, results, network, creativity.)

- What small step could you take today to move your pricing closer to your true worth?

Closing Thought

The first time I gave a quote, I was terrified they would laugh at me, and they did. But that moment taught me something I couldn't have learned any other way: If you don't value yourself, no one else will. Pricing is more than a number. It's a statement of confidence, experience, and the results you bring. And the sooner you own your worth, the sooner the right clients will too.

8
Branding, Marketing, and PR — Why They Matter More Than You Think

I've spent nearly two decades working in marketing, branding, and public relations, and if there's one thing I want you to take away from this chapter, it's that your business doesn't just survive on what you sell. It thrives or fails on how people see, hear, and remember you. That's why I couldn't write this book without giving you the real-world lessons I learned in boardrooms, on stages, in late-night strategy calls, and in mistakes that cost me more than I care to admit. My hope is that you walk away from this chapter with insights that can save you years of trial and error.

People don't just buy products or services. They buy stories, feelings, and trust. And whether you realize it or not, you're already telling a story with your business. Is it the one you want people to hear?

Early on in my career, I realized that appearances

matter, sometimes more than they should. Your age, your race, your background, or whether you have connections in the industry can change how people perceive you before you ever open your mouth. When I started my first company, people dismissed me instantly. To them, I was "too young" to be credible. I've seen clients experience the opposite, being labeled "too old" to innovate, and yes, sometimes knowing the right person opens doors. Perception is very real but it isn't permanent. When you learn to brand yourself, network with intention, and consistently deliver results, those same people who once doubted you will start paying attention.

That's why branding comes first. Branding isn't your logo, tagline, or color palette, those are tools. Branding is your reputation. It is what people say about you when you're not in the room. Strong branding starts with values. Ask yourself what three words do I want my business to stand for? Reliability, innovation, community, whatever feels true to you. Then go deeper and ask, what do I want people to feel after they've worked with me or bought from me? That answer becomes your brand promise. From there, every detail matters. If you say you're detail-oriented, your invoices should never be sloppy. If you say you're reliable, your emails should be answered on time. And above all, note that, people remember stories more than slogans. A plumber who says, "I started this business because I was tired of people waiting days for help, I wanted a service where you always know when we'll show up," has built a stronger brand than any slick logo ever could.

Once you know who you are, marketing is how you share it. The key is not to be everywhere, it's to show up in the right places, consistently. A CFO cares about numbers. A bride cares about peace of mind. A parent cares about convenience. When you know who you're talking to and what matters to them, you can stop guessing and start communicating. You don't need to juggle ten platforms at once. Pick one or two channels where your audience actually is, and do them well. For a baker, that might mean Instagram. For a contractor, Google reviews and local listings will matter more. Consistency will always beat volume. A steady rhythm, done well, builds more trust than a scattered burst of activity. And once you're showing up, measure what works. If flyers flop but referrals boom, redirect your energy. Marketing works best when you treat it like a conversation, not a megaphone.

And that's where Public Relations amplifies it. Marketing is you talking about yourself. PR is when someone else does it for you. It often carries far more weight. It doesn't require a massive agency or national coverage to make a difference. Local papers, radio stations, podcasts, and blogs are always hungry for stories. Milestones like anniversaries, awards, partnerships, or even charity events can all be opportunities for coverage. Share insights, not just sales pitches. A baker can comment on holiday dessert trends, a plumber on winter pipe care. Press builds credibility and credibility builds trust. Don't underestimate testimonials. A single client review is PR, because it is someone else validating you. The trick is not to let those moments fade. Share them in proposals, feature them on your website, or even in your email signature. Over time, these signals compound into real authority.

Branding defines the story. Marketing spreads it. PR validates it. Together, they don't just help your business survive, they give it staying power. As someone who has lived in this world for nearly two decades, I know that when entrepreneurs take ownership of their voice they don't just flourish, they lead.

Reflection Exercise

- What three words do you want people to use when describing your business?

- Where does your ideal customer spend time, and are you showing up there?

- What's one PR opportunity you could create for yourself this month? (A podcast pitch, a testimonial request, a local feature?)

Closing Thought

Your branding, marketing, and PR aren't "extras" to get around to someday. They are the foundation of your reputation, your reach, and your growth. The good news is, you don't need to have it perfect. You just need to start. Each step is defining your story.

9
Documenting Your Wins

By now, you've probably read a lot about my mistakes. I've been open about the failures, the setbacks, and the hard lessons that shaped me as an entrepreneur. But it's not only about the times we stumble. It's also about the moments we get it right, the progress we make, and the strength we discover in ourselves when we least expect it.

Success isn't measured by how many hours you work or how many tasks you cross off. Real success is learning to pause long enough to recognize your own growth and to look back at the path you've already walked and allow yourself to feel proud of how far you've come.

Entrepreneurship has a sneaky way of pulling your focus forward, always onto the next client, the next deadline, the next idea. In that cycle, you forget to look back. But entrepreneurship is emotional. There are days when you'll feel unstoppable, and others when you'll feel like you're drowning in doubt. That's why documenting your wins matters so much. They become proof when your mind tells you lies like, "You're not good enough. You're not moving fast enough." A written record shows you that progress is real.

Just over a year into my business, I was about to land one of my biggest clients when they asked me for a portfolio. I didn't have one. So I stayed up all night pulling together every campaign, every event, every client win from that whirlwind year. And when I finished, I sat back, exhausted but wide awake, staring at proof of everything I had built. For the first time, I allowed myself to feel proud.

The problem was, I didn't give myself that gift often enough. Most of the time, I was already sprinting toward the next pitch or the next fire to put out. I didn't pause to celebrate progress. Something I wish I had understood sooner is that we have to stop the glorification of "busy." Being busy is not a badge of honor. It's not proof of your worth as an entrepreneur. Hustling without stopping doesn't make you stronger, it makes you burn out.

Wins come in all sizes. Some are unforgettable, the first big client, your first employee, the moment your story lands in the press. Others are small and quiet, sending your first invoice, surviving your first tax season, raising your prices with confidence. None of these are insignificant. They're milestones. And together, they build momentum. Progress compounds. Each win stacks on the last until one day you look back and realize you've built something extraordinary.

As my business grew, I built habits around documenting wins. At the end of every project, I'd reflect on what worked, what didn't, and on how we could improve next time. This wasn't just about me, it was about shaping a culture. By walking through the wins and challenges together, I taught my team to value reflection and to hold ourselves to high standards. Every project became more than a deliverable; it became a training ground.

If wins are proof of progress, mistakes are proof of growth. Every mistake I've made has been like a miniature college degree. They sharpen instincts, refine decision-making, and prepare you for what's next. Mistakes aren't moments of defeat, they're an important part of your education. They belong to you, and you should be proud of them.

When you take time to document both wins and lessons, you build your story. That story becomes fuel for your marketing, your PR, your pitches, your credibility. It's what makes people believe in your business and in you. On hard days, when confidence is slipping, it's what lets you say: *I've done hard things before. I can do them again.*

I truly believe that mistakes give you lessons and that wins give you direction. One shows you what not to do. The other reminds you why you're doing it. Together,

they shape the business, and the leader that you
are becoming.

Lesson from Experience

Celebrate progress, not just perfection. Document your
wins as you go, and don't hide from your mistakes. They
are your education, your badges of honor, and the proof
that you are brave enough to try.

Reflection Exercise

1. Write down five wins you've had in your business
   journey so far (big or small).

2. For each win, note what made it possible, what
   habits, actions, or decisions led to it?

3. Then write down one mistake that taught you a
   lesson you'll never forget. What did it give you that
   no classroom ever could?

Closing Thought

Don't wait until the finish line to celebrate, and don't wait
until you have a degree to acknowledge the education

you've earned. Every win is a milestone, every mistake is a lesson, and both are proof that you're growing. You're already further than you were yesterday and that is worth honoring.

10
Starting From Experience

Every story has a closing chapter, and this one is mine. Saying goodbye to my first business was one of the hardest things I've ever had to do. It wasn't just a company, it was a dream, a part of me, and a place where I poured my energy, my creativity, and so many years of my life. Letting go felt, at first, like losing a piece of myself.

But endings are never really just endings. They are beginnings in disguise. That business taught me more than I could have ever imagined. It gave me confidence when I had none, strength when I felt like giving up, and lessons that no degree or textbook could have provided. It showed me that I was capable of things the younger version of myself wouldn't have even dared to dream. It shaped me into someone who not only survived the challenges of entrepreneurship, but grew from them.

There was a glorious moment when I realized I was no longer stuck in the messy middle, that space where you're fighting just to keep things afloat, unsure if it will all work out. After years of trial, error, mistakes, and constant learning, it finally clicked. The lessons had worked. My business wasn't just surviving anymore, it was thriving. It was something to be proud of. Others took note. Clients, competitors, even peers in the industry could see what I had built. And eventually, I reached the incredible milestone of being able to sell it. That moment, standing there knowing I had built something valuable enough for others to want it, was nothing short of amazing. And it was possible because of every single mistake and lesson along the way. The stumbles hadn't broken me; they had carried me.

Walking away didn't mean failure, it meant opportunities for new growth. It meant recognizing that sometimes, the chapter you're in has run its course, and it's time to turn the page. And even though a three-year non-compete agreement forced me to take a step back, it also gave me something I hadn't had in years. It gave me the space to breathe, space to reflect and space to ask myself what I really wanted next.

In that pause, I discovered something powerful. The business I had built, the mistakes I had made, the wins I had celebrated weren't gone. They had become part of me. I realized I wasn't starting over from scratch, even if it felt that way at times. I was starting again from experience.

And what a gift that is.

When the time finally came for me to begin again, I didn't walk into it alone. I carried the encouragement of my friends, the belief of my family, and the unwavering support of clients who reminded me why I loved this work in the first place. That community lifted me, encouraged me, and gave me the courage to step back into entrepreneurship with a heart that was wiser, stronger, and more resilient than before.

So this is where my story comes full circle. I said goodbye to a business that built me, and I opened the door to one I am even more proud of today. And I can say, with every ounce of certainty in me: I did not start from zero. I started from experience.

But this book isn't just about me, it's about you. You've walked through these pages, read about my mistakes, seen the lessons I've learned, and hopefully taken pieces you can carry into your own journey. I want you to feel proud for finishing this book, because what you've done here is invest in yourself. You've chosen to learn, to reflect, and to prepare yourself for the challenges and victories that lie ahead.

I hope my experiences remind you that you are not alone, that the doubts you feel are normal, and that the setbacks you face are not the end of your story. They are simply lessons, just like mine were. And just like me, you can take every single one of them and turn them into something powerful.

So as you close this chapter, I want you to know that I believe in you. I believe in your ability to take risks, to stumble, to rise again, and to create something remarkable. I believe you have what it takes to not just start, but to keep going, even when it feels hard. I believe you can do this.

And one day, when you look back on your own journey, I hope you'll feel the same sense of pride I feel now, that you didn't start from nothing. You started from experience.

And that is the best realization of all.

Dedication

I dedicate this book to you.

To the part of you that keeps showing up even when it's hard. The part that questions, rebuilds, and chooses to keep going after every setback. You know what it means to fall and still stand again. You've learned that progress rarely looks perfect, and that the real lessons are hidden inside the moments you once wished had gone differently.

I also dedicate it to the 21-year-old who didn't know it couldn't be done. The one who leapt without a plan, trusted instinct over certainty, and taught me that courage often comes before confidence. Those early missteps and bold beginnings became the foundation of everything that followed.

Through every version that's existed since, the one that doubted, the one that hoped, the one that refused to quit, I've come to understand that experience isn't just a teacher; it's the transformation itself. Every mistake held meaning. Every detour carried direction. Every fall revealed a path forward.

So this is for you, the resilient, relentless, ever-evolving soul who turns mistakes into momentum. May these pages remind you that your story, in all its imperfect beauty, is already proof that you're capable of beginning again.

About the Author

Melissa Guenette Mason is a seasoned entrepreneur and brand strategist with nearly two decades of experience helping people and businesses get seen, heard, and remembered. As the founder and CEO of A-List Media Solutions, she leads a dynamic experiential marketing and public relations agencies, known for crafting immersive brand activations, influencer events, and media strategies that turn stories into powerful experiences.

Through A-List Media Solutions, she's helped business leaders and corporations strengthen their brands, gain national media exposure, and build lasting connections with their audiences. Her campaigns don't just generate buzz, they build reputation, loyalty, and trust.

Before founding A-List Media Solutions, Melissa built and sold one of North America's top marketing and PR firms, earning firsthand insight into the triumphs and challenges of entrepreneurship. Those lessons, earned through two decades of real-world experience, became the foundation for her debut book, *Start From*

Experience, a candid and practical guide to building a business with resilience, confidence, and purpose.

Today, Melissa continues to elevate voices, shape brands, and create meaningful experiences that help others step into their spotlight, on their own terms.

thank you

You made it!

Thank you for being here, for turning each page, and for allowing me to share these stories and lessons with you. My hope is that somewhere along the way, something in these chapters made you feel seen, understood, or a little less alone on your own journey.

Writing this book has been personal and meaningful. Knowing it's found its way into your hands means more than you know. If it brought you value or encouragement, I'd love for you to share that experience with others through a short review on Amazon or Goodreads. No matter where you are in your journey, I hope you keep building, learning, and finding your own version of success, one lesson at a time.

Here's to your next chapter, to the lessons you'll gather, and to everything you'll build from experience.

Sincerely,

M.G.Mason
Melissa Guenette Mason

My Gift to You

I'm beyond thrilled that you're here!

As my gift to you, get FREE access to
the audiobook of *Start From Experience*
by scanning the QR Code below or by visiting
MelissaGuenetteMason.com